C000002835

The Essential

Civil Servant

The Essential

Civil Servant

Edited by
SIMON PETHERICK

ROBERT HALE · LONDON

© Simon Petherick 1994
First published in Great Britain 1994

ISBN 0 7090 5218 9

Robert Hale Limited
Clerkenwell House
Clerkenwell Green
London EC1R 0HT

2 4 6 8 10 9 7 5 3 1

Photoset in North Wales by
Derek Doyle & Associates, Mold, Clwyd.
Printed and bound in Hong Kong by
Bookbuilders Limited.

Preface

Civil servants are like the weather and the government of the day – everyone has an opinion about them. The opinion is often uncomplimentary, which is a fact of life that most civil servants come to accept with time; just as they realize that they will never feature as the heroes in romantic novels or as the stars on prime-time TV chat shows.

In fact, as the great Sir Edward Bridges made clear, civil servants are quite capable of dealing with public perceptions of their role; it could be said that this *sang-froid* is the characteristic that best defines them.

But there are limits. Not many civil servants would agree with Erasmus on the three qualifications of a good civil servant: 'that he should be faithful, ugly and fierce'. At least, they probably wouldn't agree on all three.

Instead, most would agree with the principle laid down in the Old Testament, that 'there is safety where there are many counsellors' (Proverbs). Safety for whom, the cynic might ask?

As the selections in this volume show, there is a general consensus around the world about the civil servant. Holding public office, no matter how lowly, will always bring with it a measure of public ribbing. But beneath the wit, there is usually the tacit recognition of the value of the civil servant, whether he be a postman or an ambassador. Somehow, life in any country seems less manageable without civil servants.

But then, they would say that, wouldn't they?

Simon Petherick

Acknowledgments

Thanks are due to the following for permission to
include copyright material: David Higham Associates for an extract from *The Castle Diaries 1974–76*
by Barbara Castle; John Murray for an extract from
Parkinson's Law by C. Northcote Parkinson; the
Daily Mirror for a quotation from Cassandra's
column; C.H. Sisson for two extracts from his work
The Spirit of the British Administration and one
from his poem *The London Zoo*, which is included in
his *Collected Poems* published by Carcanet Press;
William Heinemann Ltd for an extract from *Flight
to Arras* by Antoine de Saint Exupery; BBC
Enterprises Ltd for an extract from *Yes Prime
Minister* edited by Jonathan Lynn and Anthony Jay;
the estate of the late Sonia Brownell Orwell and
Martin Secker and Warburg Ltd for an extract from
The Lion and the Unicorn by George Orwell;
Random House Inc. for an extract from *Sex, Death
and Money* by Gore Vidal; John Calder (Publishers)
Ltd and The Calder Educational Trust, London, for
an extract from *The Killer* by Eugene Ionescu; Allen
and Unwin for an extract from *The Roads to
Freedom* by Bertrand Russell; The Society of
Authors for an extract from *Looking Back* by

Norman Douglas; Michael Joseph for an extract from *The Time of my Life* by Denis Healey; Hamish Hamilton for *Diaries of a Cabinet Minister* by Richard Crossman; Mrs Laura Huxley and Chatto and Windus for an extract from *Beyond the Mexique Bay* by Aldous Huxley; Oxford University Press for an extract from *The Lady's Not For Burning* by Christopher Fry; Peters Fraser and Dunlop for an extract from *The Anatomy of Britain* and an extract from *The New Anatomy of Britain*, both by Anthony Sampson; the estate of Adolf Hitler, the estate of Ralph Mannheim and Hutchinson Books for an extract from *Mein Kampf* by Adolf Hitler; David Higham Associates and Hodder and Stoughton for an extract from *The Spy Who Came in from The Cold* by John Le Carré; Constable for an extract from *The Crime of Galileo* by George Santayana; William Heinemann Ltd for an extract from *Time For A Tiger* by Anthony Burgess; The Society of Authors for one extract each from *Misalliance, The Apple Cart* and *Maxims for Revolutionists* by Bernard Shaw; Random House UK Ltd for an extract from *The Devil's Alternative* by Frederick Forsyth; Thomas Nelson and Sons Ltd for an extract from *Studies in the Public Records* by V.H. Galbraith.

Every effort has been made to seek permission for copyright material, and any omissions from this acknowledgments section will be remedied in any forthcoming edition.

When things haven't gone well for you, call in a
secretary or a staff man and chew him out. You
will sleep better and they will appreciate the
attention.

LYNDON BAINES JOHNSON
US President

Some civil servants are neither servants nor
civil.

WINSTON CHURCHILL (1874–1965)

Running a civil service organization is like playing an organ – you can do anything with it.

ANTHONY SAMPSON
The Anatomy of Britain

It is one of the happiest characteristics of this glowing country that official utterances are invariably regarded as unanswerable.

W. S. GILBERT (1836–1911)
collaborator with Sir Arthur Sullivan

It is alleged, indeed, that the high heels are most agreeable to our ancient constitution, but, however that may be, his majesty has determined to make use only of low heels in the administration.

JONATHAN SWIFT (1667–1745)
Gulliver's Travels, 1726

I hold here an office merely, and no opinion.

FRIEDRICH VON SCHILLER (1775–1854)

Some insomniacs take this or that potion. Our favourite soporific is the announcement by some official that this or that department will be run without regard to politics.

FRANKLIN P. ADAMS (1881–1960)

Administration, *n*. An ingenious abstraction in politics, designed to receive the kicks and cuffs due to the premier or president.

AMBROSE BIERCE (1842–*c*. 1914)
The Devil's Dictionary

I confidently expect that we shall continue to be grouped with mothers-in-law and Wigan Pier as one of the recognized objects of ridicule.

SIR EDWARD BRIDGES
lecture at the University of Cambridge, 1950

It is not without significance that most of the provisions of the Bill of Rights are procedural. It is procedure that spells much of the difference between rule by law and rule by whim or caprice.

WILLIAM O. DOUGLAS
US Supreme Court Justice

Bureaucracy is a giant mechanism operated by pygmies.

HONORÉ DE BALZAC (1799–1850)

The perfect bureaucrat everywhere is the man who manages to make no decisions and escape all responsibility.

BROOKS ATKINSON
Once Around the Sun

Every time I fill a vacant office, I make ten malcontents and one ingrate.

LOUIS XIV OF FRANCE (1638–1715)

I never have and never will (I hope) do anything for the sake of popularity; he that steers by any other compass than his own sense of duty may be a popular, but cannot be an honest, and I think not a useful public servant.

JOHN WILSON CROKER (1780–1857)
1816

A renunciation of glory and fame should be made for the public advantage.

MARCUS TULLIUS CICERO (106–43 BC)

Every man who does not go to war must work for the emperor, without reward, for a certain time.

GENGIS KHAN
Mongol Emperor (1162–1227)

We must remember that the machinery of government would not work if it were not allowed a little play in the joints.

OLIVER WENDELL HOLMES JR (1809–94)

Then give humility a coach and six,
Justice a conqueror's sword, or truth a gown,
Or public spirit its great cure, a crown.

ALEXANDER POPE (1688–1744)
Essay on Man, 1733–4

13

A politician or a civil servant is still to me an arrogant fool until he is proved otherwise.

NEVIL SHUTE (1899–1960)

The only thing that saves us from the bureaucracy is inefficiency. An efficient bureaucracy is the greatest threat to liberty.

EUGENE J. McCARTHY
in *Time* magazine, 1979

Public officials are not a group apart. They inevitably reflect the moral tune of the society in which they live.

JOHN F. KENNEDY (1917–63)
US President

What I say is, 'Thank God for the Civil Service.'

GEORGE VI (1895–1952)
to Aneurin Bevan in 1945

The Civil Service is a bit like a Rolls Royce – you know it's the best machine in the world, but you're not quite sure what to do with it.

R.A. BUTLER
British politician

14

A lot of top businesspeople become totally frustrated when they move into a cabinet position or as head of a department. They're used to much more power in business ... In government they must suddenly follow strict procedures and regulations. It's a difficult adjustment.

GERALD FORD
US President

It's getting harder and harder to support the government in the style to which it has become accustomed.

FARMER'S ALMANAC

Well-meaning, over-civilized men, in dark suits and black felt hats, with neatly rolled umbrellas crooked over the left forearm.

GEORGE ORWELL (1903–50)
on the inhabitants of Whitehall *c*. 1920, in
The Lion and the Unicorn, 1941

I do not rule Russia; ten thousand clerks do.

NICHOLAS I OF RUSSIA (1796–1855)

No government has ever been, or can ever be, wherein time-servers and blockheads will not be uppermost.

JOHN DRYDEN (1631–1700)

Every bureaucracy seeks to increase the superiority of the professionally informed by keeping their knowledge and intentions secret.

MAX WEBER

The Civil Service Entrance examinations are unavoidable for anyone trying to join the civil service. Based on the results, the Treasury has first choice of the cream, which enables that department to foul up the British economy with impeccable references.

FREDERICK FORSYTH
The Devil's Alternative

Members of the Civil Service preserved a cloak of anonymity and a tradition of discreet silence which concealed from the rest of the country the fact that they were running it.

'SIR HUMPHREY APPLETON'
Yes, Prime Minister
edited by Jonathan Lynn and Anthony Jay

Pension: An allowance made to anyone without an equivalent. In England it is generally understood to mean pay given to a state hireling for treason to his country.

SAMUEL JOHNSON (1709–84)
Dictionary, 1755

Overbearing HEO, 'You're late Jones. Get
out and come back at the proper time.'

Everybody must be managed. Queens must be managed; kings must be managed; for men want managing almost as much as women, and that's saying a good deal.

THOMAS HARDY
Under the Greenwood Tree

Let the books of the Treasury lie closed as religiously as the Sibyl's.

W.S. LANDOR
Pericles and Aspasia

Look at it from the right point of view, and there you have us – official and effectual. It's like a limited game of cricket. A field of outsiders are always going in to bowl at the Public Service, and we block the balls. Clennan asked what became of the bowlers? The airy young Barnacle replied that they grew tired, got dead beat, got lamed, got their backs broken, died off, gave it up, went in for other games.

CHARLES DICKENS
Little Dorrit

One can never find out exactly what is happening, or only a long time afterwards. We have a saying here, perhaps you have heard it: official decisions are as shy as young girls.

FRANZ KAFKA
The Castle

The Board of the Inland Revenue, which was in touch with the facts of life, introduced typewriters very shortly after they were invented ... in April 1889 [Sir Algernon West, Chairman of the Board] induced Sir Reginald [Welby, Permanent Secretary to the Treasury] to admit a carefully selected typist, with her machine, to the Treasury building. In May, another one was let in to keep the first one from pining, and then the whole Treasury sat back and confidently waited for disaster. It waited three years, but all that happened, apart from a noticeable speed up in routine business, was that in 1892 one of the old copyists retired on pension.

J.P.W. MALLALIEU
Passed To You Please, 1942

I have found a new pleasure in life travelling with a Private Secretary. One just walks about in a fur coat and things get done.

HAROLD NICOLSON (1886–1968)
Diaries and Letters, 1939–45

The public has never quite made up its mind whether to give pride of place to stupid obstructiveness or incompetent laziness in its assessment of their [civil servants'] character.

C.K. MUNRO
The Fountains in Trafalgar Square, 1952

There is no government without mumbo–jumbo.

HILAIRE BELLOC (1870–1953)

Government defines the physical aspects of man by means of The Printed Form, so that for every man in the flesh there is an exactly corresponding man on paper.

JEAN GIRAUDOUX (1882–1944)
The Enchanted

Government is the only agency that can take a useful commodity like paper, slap some ink on it, and make it totally worthless.

LUDWIG EDLER VON MISES

We weed out the darnel from the corn and the unfit in war, but do not excuse evil men from the service of the state.

ANTISTHENES (444–365 BC)

Public servants: persons chosen by the people to distribute the graft.

MARK TWAIN (1835–1910)

A prince who is himself not wise cannot be well advised.

> NICCOLO MACHIAVELLI (1469–1527)
> *The Prince*, 1513

I think we have more machinery of government than is necessary, too many parasites living on the labour of the industrious.

> THOMAS JEFFERSON (1743–1826)
> US President

The Civil Service is a self-perpetuating oligar-
chy, and what better system is there?

LORD ARMSTRONG

Here is £600 a year for doing nothing, and you
are just the man to do it.

LORD DERBY
to Charles Lever, when he was appointed
Consul at Trieste in 1873

The perfect civil servant is the man who has a
valid objection to any possible solution.

A.H. KEATES
speech to the Institute of Hospital Manage-
ment, 1965

A civil servant is a faceless mortal riding like a
flea on the back of the dog, Legislation.

ANON
quoted in *The Wit of the Civil Service*, ed.
E. Inglis

A dog's obeyed in office.

WILLIAM SHAKESPEARE (1564–1616)
Othello, 1604

To be governed is to be watched, inspected, spied upon, directed, law–ridden, regulated, penned up, indoctrinated, preached at, checked, appraised, seized, censured, commanded, by beings who have neither title, nor knowlege, nor virtue.

P.J. PROUDHON (1809–65)

Public bureaucracy breeds private bureaucracy ... The more government expands, the more it stimulates a vast supporting apparatus of trade associations, lawyers, lobbyists, research groups, economists and consultants.

PAUL A. SAMUELSON
in the *Washington Post*

Of hundreds of governors sent from London to Australasia, perhaps ten or a dozen were decent civil servants who tried to do their best. All the rest were brainless duffers or worse ... quite ordinary little men who earnestly strove to ape the manners and methods of royalty and create a mimic court.

GEORGE DICK MEUDELL
The Pleasant Career of a Spendthrift

Too bad that all the people who know how to run the country are busy driving taxicabs and cutting hair.

GEORGE BURNS

Nothing beyond the State, above the State, against the State. Everything to the State, for the State, in the State.

BENITO MUSSOLINI (1883–1945)

An administration, like a machine, does not create. It carries on.

ANTOINE DE SAINT–EXUPÉRY (1900–44)
Flight to Arras, 1942

No inanimate thing will move from one place to another without a piece of paper that goes along telling someone where to move it.

CHARLES E. WILSON
American government official, 1952

In a country where the sole employer is the State, opposition means death by slow starvation.

LEON TROTSKY (1879–1941)

We are governed by a Civil Service which has such enormous power that its regulations are taking the place of the laws of England, though some of them are made for the convenience of the officials without the slightest regard for the convenience or even the rights of the public.

GEORGE BERNARD SHAW (1856–1950)
The Apple Cart, 1929

As it was in the beginning
Is to-day official sinning
And shall be for evermore.

RUDYARD KIPLING (1865–1936)
Departmental Ditties, 1886

[The UK civil servant travelling abroad was] shocked to discover that many countries are administered by men who read books about public administration. Such people were committing the crime of learning from books something one just does. It is rather like venturing into matrimony only after a course of Havelock Ellis which, for a healthy nature, should not be strictly necessary.

C.H. SISSON (1914–)
The Spirit of British Administration

[The civil servant] should be prepared to bow before any wisdom whose mouth is loud enough.

C.H. SISSON (1914–)

ibid.

The besetting sin of civil servants is to mix too much with each other.

SIR WILLIAM BEVERIDGE

The nearest thing to immortality in this world is a government bureau.

GENERAL HUGH S. JOHNSON

Our greatest growth industry is the Civil Service.

LORD LUCAS (1896–1967)

Committees are the oriflamme of democracy.

HAROLD MACMILLAN

The minister exists to tell the Civil Servant what the public will not stand.

SIR WILLIAM HARCOURT (1827–1904)

Take care of the pence and the pounds will take care of themselves.

WILLIAM LOWNDES (1695–1724)
Treasury Secretary

Always remember that if a civil servant has the ability to … correctly foresee the demand situation for any product he would not be working for the government for long. He would shortly be sitting in the south of France with his feet in a bucket of champagne!

BERT KELLY
Economics Made Easy

The state, it cannot too often be repeated, does nothing, and can give nothing, which it does not take from somebody.

HENRY GEORGE (1839–97)

Farming looks mighty easy when your plough is a pencil, and you're a thousand miles from the corn field.

DWIGHT D. EISENHOWER (1890–1969)
US President

The noblest motive is the public good.

SIR RICHARD STEELE (1672–1729)
The Spectator, vol. 3, 200, 1744

Civilization declines in relation to the increase in bureaucracy.

VICTOR YANNACONE
Sports Illustrated

When a king creates an office, Providence creates immediately a fool to buy it.

COLBERT

It seems to me that our responsible public officials should be doing more important things than writing Federal specifications for panty-hose or the size of lettering on a can of sardines.

MAX E. BRUNK
Cornell University

This judgment I have of you, that you will not be corrupted by any manner of gift and that you will be faithful to the State, and that without respect of my private will, you will give me that counsel that you think best.

> ELIZABETH I (1533–1603)
> on Sir William Cecil, Secretary of State, 1558

Britain has invented a new missile. It's called the civil servant – it doesn't work and it can't be fired.

> GENERAL SIR WALTER WALKER
> in *The Observer*, 1981

Wherefore the Little Tin Gods harried their
    little tin souls,
Seeing he came not from Chatham, jingled no
    spurs at his heels,
Knowing that, nevertheless, was he first on
    the Government rolls,
For the billet of 'Railway Instructor to Little
    Tin Gods on Wheels'.

> RUDYARD KIPLING (1865–1936)
> *Public Waste*

This place needs a laxative.

> BOB GELDOF
> on the European Commission

The business of a civil servant is to do as he is told.

SIR FRANCIS MOWATT

I think some of our government departments should see about getting themselves more appropriate names. Our military ministry, seeing we are neutral, should be called the Department of the Fence. And surely the Department of Agriculture is a poor title – would it not be better to call it the Department of Yokel Government?

FLANN O'BRIEN (1911–66)

Public bodies are so far worse than the individuals composing them, because the *official* takes place of the *moral sense*.

WILLIAM HAZLITT (1778–1830)
On Corporate Bodies

Do remember that the speed of the bureaucratic machine makes British Rail look like Concorde.

JEFFREY ARCHER
First Among Equals

It's all papers and forms, the entire Civil Service is like a fortress made of papers, forms and red tape.

ALEXANDER OSTROVSKY (1823–86)
The Diary of a Scoundrel

An ambassador is an honest man sent to lie abroad for the commonwealth.

SIR HENRY WOTTON (1568–1639)
In an Album, 1604

The inseparable imperfection annexed to all human governments consisted, he said, in not being able to create a sufficient fund of virtue and principle to carry the laws into due and effectual execution. Wisdom might plan, but virtue alone could execute. And where could sufficient virtue be found? A variety of delegated, and often discretionary, powers must be entrusted somewhere; which, if not governed by integrity and conscience, would necessarily be abused, till at last the constable would sell his for a shilling.

JAMES BOSWELL (1740–95)
Life of Samuel Johnson, 1791

Good counsellors lack no clients.

WILLIAM SHAKESPEARE (1564–1616)
Measure For Measure, 1604

The State is a collection of officials, different for different purposes, drawing comfortable incomes so long as the status quo is preserved. The only alteration they are likely to desire in the status quo is an increase of bureaucracy and of the power of the bureaucrats.

BERTRAND RUSSELL (1872–1970)
Maurice Conaway lecture, 1922

His heart was at his office, his heart was always there, A-docketing the papers and minuting with care.

CHARLES KNIGHT (1791–1873)
London, 1841–4

The civil servant is not to consider the purpose of what he does, nor even to engage in any activity resembling an expression of political commitment, lest he think about the purposes to which he daily contributes his talents.

> SUSANNAH LESSARD
> *Washington Monthly*, 1971

'Muddlington' with a high standard of honour and a low standard of efficiency is the dominant note of Australian Public Life. With more careful selection in its civil service, and better trained intelligence in its public men, the Australian Government would become a striking instance of successful democratic institutions. At present it is at least a most promising experiment.

> BEATRICE WEBB (1858–1943)
> *The Webbs' Australian Diary*

Skewered through and through with office pens, and bound hand and foot with red tape.

CHARLES DICKENS (1812–70)
David Copperfield, 1849–50

Just as the politicians at Westminster have long been convinced that the senior civil servants all wear bowler hats and old school ties or twinsets and pearls, and spend their Friday evenings at Tory party shin-digs in the suburbs, or else – according to party standpoint – go in for beards, unisex jeans, and secret conclaves with militants from Islington, so the mandarins insist that for them the ideal minister is one who knows his mind and how to get his way in Cabinet even when they think he's wrong.

JOCK BRUCE-GARDYNE
Minister and Mandarins

Humanity will not be happy until the last capitalist is hanged with the guts of the last bureaucrat.

Graffiti during the Paris riots of 1968

There is no worse heresy than that the office sanctifies the holder of it.

FIRST BARON ACTON (1834–1902)
letter to Bishop Mandell Creighton, 1887

Bad administration, to be sure, can destroy good policy; but good administration can never save bad policy.

ADLAI EWING STEVENSON (1900–65)

The only governments, not representative, in which high political skill and ability have been other than exceptional, whether under monar- chical or aristocratic forms, have been essen- tially bureaucracies. The work of government has been in the hands of governors by profession; which is the essence and meaning of bureaucracy.

JOHN STUART MILL (1806–73)
Representative Government, 1861

Nothing doth more hurt in a state than that cunning men pass for wise.

FRANCIS BACON (1561–1626)
Of Cunning

41

The State … is the most flagrant negation, the most cynical and complete negation of humanity.

MIKHAIL BAKUNIN (1814–1876)

One generally feels a sort of diffidence in introducing one's self; but I may remark that I was at that time a Government official, of the ninth class; paid rather according to my grade than my merit, and not by any means in proportion to the loafing I had to do.

JOSEPH FURPHY
Such Is Life

Civil servants have many good qualities but when it comes to running businesses they tend, albeit for reasons largely outside their control, to be disastrous failures.

LESLIE CHAPMAN
Your Disobedient Servant

The best servants of the people, like the best valets, must whisper unpleasant truth's in the master's ear.

WALTER LIPPMANN
Some Necessary Iconoclasm: A Preface to Politics

There is, or should be, no role in our society for people with little to offer in a practical way, but civil servants have got round this stumbling block by inventing a role for themselves.

BRIAN SEDGEMORE
1977

For whom thy labour all done is,
And hast made all they rekenings,
Instead of rest and of new things,
Thou goest home to thine house anone,
And all so dombe as anie stone,
Thou sittest at another booke,
Till fully dazed is thy looke.

> WILLIAM CHAUCER
> *House of Fame*

If you do anything well, gratitude is lighter than a feather; if you have done anything wrong, the people's wrath is heavy as lead.

> TITUS MAGGIUS PLAUTUS (*c.* 254–184 BC)
> *Poenulus*

Here comes Mr. Winter, collector of taxes;
I'd advise you to pay him whatever he axes;
Excuses won't do; he stands no sort of
    flummery,
Though Winter his name is, his process is
    summary.

> THEODORE HOOK

Humanism with the sap dried out of it.

> SIR MICHAEL SADLER
> on the Civil Service mentality

A copier must always work mind, eye and hand together. He can't talk to other folk, or sing, and lark. We labour in silence, stoop and stare on the sheepskin. Our copying hurts our stomachs, our backs and our eyes. Anyone who has copied for twenty years like I have suffers for it in every bit of his body.

> OCCLEVE, poet
> on 35 years in the Privy Seal Office

The bureaucracy is what we all suffer from.

> OTTO VON BISMARCK (1815–98)
> 1891

The smugglers being grown to such a degree of insolence, as to carry on their wicked practices by force and violence, not only in the country and the remote parts of the Kingdom, but even in the City of London itself, going in gangs armed with swords, pistols and other weapons, even to the number of forty or fifty, by which means they have been too strong, not only for the officers of the Revenue but for the civil magistrates themselves ... The number of Custom House officers who have been beaten, abused and wounded since Christmas 1723 being no less than 250, besides six others who have been actually murdered in the execution of their duty.

> Parliamentary Inquiry into the smuggling
> trade, 1736

Of government officials, there are not a few in New South Wales; they enjoy, for the most part, I may say throughout, very comfortable salaries, and as a rule, I think there is no alarming percentage of sufferers from overwork among them.

GEORGE LACON JAMES
Shall I Try Australia?

A class of inferior officers belonging to the Customs and Excise including what are called 'Supernumaries' and 'Glutmen', many of whom connive at pillage as well as frauds committed on the Revenue, and share in the plunder to a very considerable extent; principally from their inability to support themselves on the pittance allowed them in the name of salary.

COLQUHOUN
Treatise on the Police in London, 1796

Civil servants are too often regarded by the public as a body of soul-less bureaucrats, whose only pleasure in life consists in devising harassing regulations to restrict our personal liberty. My own experience leads me to think differently.

HRH PRINCE GEORGE, 1930

The functionaries of every government have propensities to command at will the liberty and property of their constituents.

THOMAS JEFFERSON (1743–1826)
US President

I object to having tons of papers which are never opened sent to my lodgings. I have been out of town for a few weeks, and on my return, instead of being able to go to the Derby I had to wade through a mass of Parliamentary papers. I put away 1lb and threw away about 2cwt. I could not sell the residue; I could not exchange them for books, for that would be selling them; I could not burn them, for that would be voted a nuisance. Why should these tons of paper be thrust on unwilling members?

V. SCULLY,
MP for Cork County, in Commons debate on
Civil Service Estimates, 1865

Recommendations of Committees, however wise and strongly urged, are of little use, more especially when clashing with vested interests, unless some Department or individual is responsible for carrying them into effect.

HENRY FOWLER
British Politician
1887

Idle clerical officer to diligent friend, 'All work and no play, y'know. Why don't you have a weekend at brighton?'

'I tried that but the waitress took all my change and the hotel bill took the rest!'

There seems to be little, if any, feeling in Australia that there are some matters which should be beyond the reach of politicians or bureaucrats.

ROBERT MARSDEN HOPE

Bureaucracy defends the status quo long past the time when the quo has lost its status.

DR LAURENCE J. PETER
Canadian educator

I have so often wandered through these gloomy passages without finding a sign of humanity there – without hearing any slightest tick of the hammer of labour, that I am disposed to think that Lord Chancellors have been anxious to save their subordinates from suicide, and have mercifully decreed that the whole staff of labourers, down to the very message boys of the office, should be sent away to green fields or palatial clubs during, at any rate, a moiety of their existence.

ANTHONY TROLLOPE (1815–82)
Can You Forgive Her?, 1864

A man is badly in need of advice when he has many advisers.

PUBLILIUS SYRUS (first century BC)

The speed of exit of a civil servant is directly proportional to the quality of his service.

RALPH NADER
The Spoiled System

The insolence of office.

WILLIAM SHAKESPEARE (1564–1616)
Hamlet

Mr Cooling, my Lord Chamberlain's secretary
… proved very drunk, and did talk … [and] told
us his horse was a Bribe, and his boots a bribe;
and told us he was made up of bribes … and
invited me home to his house, to taste of his
bribe-wine.

SAMUEL PEPYS (1633–1703)
Diary, 30 July 1667

Meetings are indispensable when you don't
want to do anything.

J.K. GALBRAITH (1908–   )
Ambassador's Journal

It may pass for a maxim in the State, that the administration cannot be placed in too few hands, nor the legislature in too many.

JONATHAN SWIFT (1667–1745)

For the administration of the government, like the office of a trustee, must be conducted for the benefit of those entrusted to one's care, not of those to whom it is entrusted.

MARCUS TULLIUS CICERO (106–43 BC)
De Officiis

Large organization is loose organization. Nay, it would be almost as true to say that organization is always disorganization.

G.K. CHESTERTON (1874–1936)
Outline of Sanity

Who cannot give good counsel? 'Tis cheap, it costs them nothing.

ROBERT BURTON (1577–1640)
The Anatomy of Melancholy, 1621

What constitutes a State?
Not high-crown'd battlement or labour'd mound,
Thick wall or moated gate;
Not cities proud with spires and turrets crown'd;
No: – men, high-minded men,
Men who their duties know,
But know their rights, and, knowing, dare maintain
These constitute a State.

SIR WILLIAM JONES (1746–94)
An Ode in Imitation of Alcoeus

Thence to Whitehall and there a Committee met, where little was done.

SAMUEL PEPYS (1633–1703)
Diary, 30 September 1667

He who administers governs.
MATTHEW ARNOLD (1822–88)

Australians have a characteristic talent for bureaucracy.

ALAN FRASER DAVIES
Australian Democracy

A basic rule of bureaucracies: the longer the title, the lower the rank.

HUGH RAWSON
A Dictionary of Euphemisms

A civil servant doesn't make jokes.

EUGÈNE IONESCU (1912–)
The Killer

Bureaucracy is not an obstacle to democracy but an inevitable complement to it.

JOSEPH SCHUMPETER
Capitalism, Socialism and Democracy

A man may govern the Mandarins, and yet live in comparative idleness. To do such governing work well a man should have a good presence, a flow of words which should mean nothing, an excellent temper, and a love of hospitality.

ANTHONY TROLLOPE (1815–82)
He Knew He Was Right, 1869

The culminating point of administration is to know well how much power, great or small, we ought to use in all circumstances.

BARON DE MONTESQUIEU (1689–1755)

When one sees some of the human specimens which the mills of the Civil Service grind out for our governance, when one finds oneself at the mercy of boors who occupy responsible posts only because they had a mathematical or historical link, or a mere knack of passing examinations – why, then one cannot help thinking that there is something to be said for Lord Palmerston's point of view.

NORMAN DOUGLAS (1868–1952)
Looking Back
Lord Palmerston thought appointment to civil service posts should be by patronage

Bad officials are elected by good citizens who do not vote.

GEORGE JEAN NATHAN (1882–1958)

Nowadays, for the sake of the advantage which is to be gained from the public revenues and from office, men want to be always in office.

ARISTOTLE (384–322 BC)
Politics

While the state exists there is no freedom; when there is no freedom there will be no state.

    VLADIMIR ILICH LENIN (1870–1924)
    The State and the Revolution

Men who are engaged in settling difficult questions should be devoid of hatred, of friendship, of anger, and of soft heartedness.

    SALLUST (86–35 BC)
    The Conspiracy of Catiline

Every governmental institution has been a standing testimony to the harmonic destiny of society, a standing proof that the life of man is destined for peace and amity, instead of disorder and contention.

    HENRY JAMES (1843–1916)

Big brother is watching you.

GEORGE ORWELL (1903–1950)
1984, 1949

How self-government has to be worked out and how one can manage without bureaucracy … is still shown in Australia, Canada, and the other English colonies.

FRIEDRICH ENGELS (1820–95)
Critique of the Social-Democratic Draft Programme, 1891

Fortune often makes up for the eminence of office by the inferiority of the officeholder.

BALTASAR GRACIAN
The Art of Worldly Wisdom, 1647

All Treasurers, if they do good service to their masters, must be generally hated.

JAMES I (1566–1625)

The soul of our service is the loyalty with which we execute ordained error.

LORD VANSITTART

Lift the curtain and 'the State' reveals itself as a little group of fallible men in Whitehall, making guesses about the future, influenced by political prejudices and partisan prejudices, and working on projections drawn from the past by a staff of economists.

ENOCH POWELL

There is something about a bureaucrat that does not like a poem.

GORE VIDAL
Sex, Death and Money

Here thou, great Anna! whom three realms obey,
Dost sometimes counsel take – and sometimes tea.

ALEXANDER POPE (1688–1744)
The Rape of the Lock, 1712–14

To place and power all public spirit tends;
In place and power all public spirit ends.

THOMAS MOORE (1779–1852)
Irish Melodies, 1801–34

The bureaucracy is cancerous from head to foot;
only its stomach is healthy, and the laws it
passes as excrement are the most natural filth
in the world.

OTTO VON BISMARCK (1815–1898)

Many are wise in their own ways, that are weak for government or counsel.

FRANCIS BACON (1561–1626)

A memorandum is written not to inform the reader but to protect the writer.

DEAN ACHESON

The administration of government, like a guardianship, ought to be directed to the good of those who confer, and not of those who receive the trust.

MARCUS TULLIUS CICERO (106–43 BC)

In France there is only one thing that we cannot make: a free government; and only one thing that we cannot destroy: centralization.

ALEXIS DE TOCQUEVILLE (1805–59)
Recollections

Too many time-servers rot the State.

GEORGE MEREDITH (1828–1909)
Beauchamp's Career, 1876

The easy-going nature of the Australian ... has not protected him from the encroachment of modern bureaucracy to impose on him more easily.

JOHN PRINGLE
Australian Accent

Millions are fascinated by the plan to transform the whole world into a bureau, to make everybody a bureaucrat, and to wipe out any private initiative. The paradise of the future is visualized as an all-embracing bureaucratic apparatus ... Streams of blood have been shed for the realization of this ideal.

LUDWIG EDLER VON MISES
Bureaucracy

If you really want to get your teeth into the biggest rice pudding of all, I suggest you take a look at the duties of government and its administrative structure.

PRINCE PHILIP (1921–   )
1967

The impertinence and arrogance of the Civil Service really sticks in my gullet.

TONY BENN
Against the Tide: Diaries 1973–76

In our democracy officers of the government are the servants, and never the masters of the people.

FRANKLIN D ROOSEVELT (1882–1945)
US President
1941

A committee is a group that keeps minutes and loses hours.

MILTON BERLE
News Summaries

This struggle and scramble for office, for a way to live without work, will finally test the strength of our institutions.

ABRAHAM LINCOLN (1809–65)
US President
1861

A Government of statesmen or of clerks? Of Humbug or of Humdrum?

BENJAMIN DISRAELI (1804–81)
Coningsby, 1844

Great positions render great men still greater; small positions make little men smaller.

JEAN DE LA BRUYERE (1645–96)
De L'Homme

One thing the House will NEVER forgive and that is if a minister misleads it ... The blame is always on you and *not* on the Civil Service.

STANLEY BALDWIN (1867–1947)
in a letter to Sir John Reith, 1940

A bureaucrat's life is not a happy one (tra la!), unless he can provide increasing budgets for his subordinate bureaucrats to disburse in salaries and contracts.

WILLIAM A. NISKANEN
Bureaucracy: Servant or Master?

Bad appointments to office are a threefold inconvenience: they are an injury to public business; they dishonour the prince; and they are a kind of robbery of those who deserve advancement.

FREDERICK THE GREAT (1712–86)

Australia is, in fact, an old man's bureaucracy.

ROBIN BOYD
Artificial Australia

The civil servant wants to show that he took the right decision, gave the right advice, asked the right questions and obtained the right facts before placing the right minute before the right authority. What actually *happens* is of little consequence.

C. NORTHCOTE PARKINSON (1909–   )
In-Laws and Outlaws

I saw that the State was half-witted, that it was timid as a lone woman with her silver spoons, and that it did not know its friends from its foes, and I lost all my remaining respect for it, and pitied it.

H.D. THOREAU (1817–62)
Cape Cod

Germany was the best organized and best administered country in the world. The German government official might well be accused of bureaucratic red tape, but in the other countries things were no better in this respect; they were worse. But what the other countries did not possess was the wonderful solidity of this apparatus and the incorruptible honesty of its members.

ADOLF HITLER (1889–1945)
Mein Kampf, 1925–6

Whenever there is a great national establishment, employing large numbers of officials, the public must be reconciled to support many incompetent men; for such is the favouritism and nepotism always prevailing in the purlieus of these establishments, that some incompetent persons are always admitted, to the exclusion of many of the worthy.

HERMAN MELVILLE (1819–91)
White Jacket, 1850

An Official Thinking up a Swift and Cutting
Reply to a Tentative Inquiry.

I am quite clear that the official must be the
mainspring of the new society, suggesting,
promoting, advising at every stage ... Only the
skilled and trained official can really be relied
upon to keep continuity, system, impartial
administration, tradition, and disinterested
impetus.

SIR JOSIAH STAMP

The mystery of the State is become, like that of Godliness, ineffable and incomprehensible, and has likewise the same good luck of being thought the finer for not being understood.

FOURTH EARL OF CHESTERFIELD (1694–1773)
1716

Men who write minutes, who make professional assessments, who are never attacked face to face, who dwell in the Sargasso Sea of the Civil Service and who love the seaweed that conceals them.

CASSANDRA
Daily Mirror

I'm surprised that a government organization could do it that quickly.

JIMMY CARTER
US President
when told that it took twenty years to build the Great Pyramid of Giza

The gretteste clerkes been noght the wisest men.

GEOFFREY CHAUCER (c. 1343–1400)
The Reeve's Tale, c. 1387

Caesar's double-bed is warm
As an unimportant clerk
Writes I DO NOT LIKE MY WORK
On a pink official form.

    W.H. AUDEN (1907–73)
    The Fall of Rome

This year is the Centenary of the Income Tax. The best way to celebrate it. By our Artist, who has not yet paid his.

A bureaucracy is a continuing congregation of people who must act more or less as one.

J.K. GALBRAITH (1908–   )

The noble spirit of the metropolis is the lifeblood of the state, collected at the heart.

'JUNIUS' (*fl.* 1770)
Letters, 1769–71

For forms of government let fools contest;
Whate'er is best administered is best.

ALEXANDER POPE (1688–1744)
Essay on Man, 1733–4

So when any of the four pillars of government are mainly shaken or weakened (which are religion, justice, counsel, and treasure), men had need to pray for fair weather.

FRANCIS BACON (1561–1626)
Of Seditions and Troubles

The Treasury could not, with any marked success, run a fish and chip shop.

HAROLD WILSON (1916–   )
1984

You know the difference between leaking and briefing. Briefing is what I do and leaking is what you do.

> JAMES CALLAGHAN
> to the Franks Committee, in the *Report of the Departmental Committee on Section 2 of the Official Secrets Act 1911*

Senior civil servants at the War Office were capable of acting without delay; at lower levels, on the other hand, a love of obstruction was in places deeply rooted on the civil side.

> ANTHONY POWELL
> *Faces in my Time*

Thou dreary piles, fit mansion for a Gresham or a Whittington of old stately House of Merchants; with thy labyrinthine passages, and light-excluding pent-up offices, where candles for one half the year supplied the place of the sun's light; unhealthy contributor to my weal, stern fosterer of my living.

> CHARLES LAMB
> on East India House in *The Superannuated Man*

The men of the Internal Navigation [Office] are known to be fast, nay, almost furious, in their pace of living; not that they are extravagant in any degree, a fault which their scale of salaries very generally forbids, but they are one and all addicted to Coal Holes and Cider Cellars; they dive at midnight hours into Shades, and know all the back parlours of all the public houses in the neighbourhood of the Strand. Here they leave messages for one another, and call the girl at the bar by her Christian name. They are a set of men endowed with sallow complexions, and they wear loud clothing and spend more money in gin and in water than in gloves.

ANTHONY TROLLOPE
The Three Clerks

It was towards the end of the year 1859 that, fresh from Marlborough, I distinguished myself by gaining first place in a competition held by the Civil Service Commission for a clerkship in the Privy Council Office. Frankness compels me to add that the other two nominees may have been the special couple known as the 'Treasury Idiots' who could not pass anything and were sent up to give a walkover to any minister's protégé able to reach the minimum qualifications. At any rate, they could hardly read and write, and so I found myself entitled to a desk at Downing Street.

HERBERT PRESTON-THOMAS
The Work and Play of a Government Inspector

The more the state expands, the more liberty diminishes.

> JEAN-JACQUES ROUSSEAU (1712–78)
> *The Social Contract*, 1762

But yet beware of councils when too full; number makes long disputes.

> SIR JOHN DENHAM (1615–69)
> *Of Prudence*

A committee is a cul-de-sac down which ideas are lured and then quietly strangled.

> BARNETT COCKS
> in the *New Scientist*

The natural bureaucrat is grieved if he has to spend his own money.

> JO GRIMOND
> *The Bureaucratic Blight*

Bureaucratic function is sustained by fear or failure as the church was once supported by fear of damnation.

> RICHARD N. GOODWIN
> *The American Condition*

The committee sat and sat, till every sensible plan was crushed as flat as a pancake.

C.H. SPURGEON
Salt-Cellars

A state is never greater than when all its superfluous hands are employed in the service of the public.

DAVID HUME (1711–76)
Essays: Of Commerce

But the privilege and pleasure
That we treasure beyond measure
Is to run on little errands for the Ministers of State.

W.S. GILBERT (1836–1911)
The Gondoliers, 1889

Stalin is the most outstanding mediocrity of the Soviet bureaucracy.

LEON TROTSKY (1879–1941)

When all the fine phrases are stripped away, it appears the state is only a group of men with human interests, passions, and desires, or, worse yet, the state is only an obscure clerk hidden in some corner of a governmental bureau. In either case the assumption of superhuman wisdom and virtue is proved false.

W.G. SUMNER
Commercial Crises

Thrift should be the guiding principle in our government expenditure. It should be made clear to all government workers that corruption and waste are very great crimes.

MAO TSE-TUNG (1893–1976)
Our Economic Policy

The proposal is frequently made that the government ought to assume the risks that are 'too great for private industry'. This means that bureaucrats should be permitted to take risks with the taxpayers' money that no one is willing to take with his own.

HENRY HAZLITT

The man of narrower mind is often the better administrator.

JOSEPH RICKABY
An Old Man's Jottings

Sancho asked: 'Who here is my secretary?'
And one of those standing by answered: 'I, sir, for I can read and write, and I'm a Basque.'
'With that last qualification,' said Sancho, 'you could well be secretary to the Emperor himself.'

MIGUEL DE CERVANTES (1547–1616)
Don Quixote, 1605–15

The Treasury is a bunch of bank clerks who think they are mandarins.

LORD BELOFF

The greatest things and the most praiseworthy that can be done for the public good are not what require great parts, but great honesty.

ALEXANDER POPE (1688–1744)
Thoughts on Various Subjects

M.ʳ *Wiseman*

Nothing is easier than spending the public money. It does not appear to belong to anybody. The temptation is overwhelming to bestow it on somebody.

CALVIN COOLIDGE (1872–1933)

A clerk in a Public Office ... labours in an obscurity as profound as it is unavoidable. His official character is absorbed in that of his superior. He must devote all his talents, and all his learning, to measures, some of which he will assuredly disapprove, without having the slightest power to prevent them; and to some of which he will most essentially contribute, without having any share whatever in the credit of them. He must listen silently to praises bestowed on others, which his pain has earned for them; and if any accident should make him notorious enough to become the suspected author of any unpopular act, he must silently submit to the reproach, even though it be totally unmerited by him. These are indeed the indispensable disadvantages of the position of a clerk in a Public Office, and no man of sense and temper would complain of them. But neither will any man of real mental power, to whom the truth is known beforehand, subject himself to an arduous examination in order to win a post so ill paid, so obscure, and so subordinate or should he win it, no such man will long retain it.

SIR JAMES STEPHEN (1789–1859)
1854

When a man assumes a public trust, he should consider himself as public property.

THOMAS JEFFERSON (1743–1826)
US President

The Treasury has grown from being the guardian of the strong box to becoming the universal controller of every Department of HMG. It regards all other Departments as inferior to itself; it looks upon them as licentious spendthrifts, as prodigal sons from whose voracious maw it is the province of the Treasury to seize the fatted calf. The result is that all Departments labour under a more than Egyptian bondage.

> GIBSON BOWLES,
> British Politician
> 1900

The uniform, constant and uninterrupted effort of every man to better his condition, the principle from which public and national, as well as private opulence is originally derived, is frequently powerful enough to maintain the natural progress of things toward improvement, in spite both of the extravagance of government, and of the greatest errors of administration. Like the unknown principle of animal life, it frequently restores health and vigour to the constitution, in spite, not only of the disease, but of the absurd prescriptions of the doctor.

> ADAM SMITH
> *Wealth of Nations*

A state may prosper under any form of government, provided it is well administered.

> CLAUDE HENRI SAINT-SIMON (1675–1755)

In theory, [government] is simply a device for supplying a variable series of common needs and the men constituting it (as all ranks of them are so fond of saying) are only public servants; but in fact its main purpose is not service at all but exploitation, and the men constituting it are as little moved by concepts of public duty and responsibility as, say, the corps of advertising agents, or that of stockbrokers, or that of attorneys.

H.L. MENCKEN (1880–1956)

Public money is like holy water – everyone helps himself.

ITALIAN PROVERB

The relations between a Minister and his Secretary are, or at least should be, among the finest that can subsist between two individuals. Except the married state, there is none in which so great a confidence is involved, in which more forbearance ought to be exercised or more sympathy ought to exist.

BENJAMIN DISRAELI (1804–81)
Endymion, 1880

The number of the officials and the quantity of the work are not related to each other at all.

C. NORTHCOTE PARKINSON (1909–   )
Parkinson's Law, 1958

Government is emphatically a machine: to the discontented a 'taxing machine', to the contented a 'machine for security of property'.

THOMAS CARLYLE (1795–1881)
Signs of the Times

Lord, the money we do spend on government and it's not one bit better than the government we got for one-third the money twenty years ago.

WILL ROGERS

[The Civil Service is] an official caste ... whose whole instincts will drive them towards tyranny. Together with the natural love of power, they will have a rooted conviction that they alone know enough to be able to judge what is good for the community.

BERTRAND RUSSELL (1872–1970)
Roads to Freedom

Dullness is decent in the Church and State.

JOHN DRYDEN (1631–1700)

Washington bureaucrats have finally figured out how to balance the budget. They're going to tilt the country.

ANON

It is the anonymous 'they', the enigmatic 'they' who are in charge. Who is 'they'? I don't know. Nobody knows. Not even 'they' themselves.

JOSEPH HELLER (1923–)

He who administers governs.

MATTHEW ARNOLD (1822–88)

One to mislead the public, another to mislead the Cabinet, and the third to mislead itself.

HERBERT HENRY ASQUITH (1852–1928)
on why the War Office kept three sets of figures

There is no subtler way of flattering a retired official than to criticize his successor in office.

J.A. SPENDER
The Comments of Bagshot

Here lies a civil servant. He was civil
To everyone, and servant to the devil.

C.H. SISSON (1914–)
The London Zoo, 1961

Why are Trafalgar Square fountains like Government Clerks? – Because they play from 10 till 4.

PUNCH
17 July 1858

The State, that cawing rookery of committees and subcommittees.

V.S. PRITCHETT (1900–   )

A Ward Beadle

The Civil Service is profoundly deferential. 'Yes, Minister! No, Minister! If you wish it, Minister!'

RICHARD CROSSMAN
Diaries of a Cabinet Minister

Guidelines for bureaucrats: (1) When in charge, ponder. (2) When in trouble, delegate. (3) When in doubt, mumble.

JAMES H. BOREN
New York Times

Official dignity tends to increase in inverse ratio to the importance of the country in which office is held.

ALDOUS HUXLEY (1894–1963)
Beyond the Mexique

Prime Ministers are dispensable, but private secretaries are not.

JOHN VINCENT
The Observer

He that serves a communaltie is controlled by every one, rewarded by none.

RANDLE COTGRAVE (d. *c.* 1634)
Dictionary: Abbayer

The zealous official, who does not care what is done so long as he is at the centre of it.

WINSTON CHURCHILL (1874–1965)
on Sunderland, *Marlborough*, vol. 1

It is not easy nowadays to remember anything so contrary to appearances as that officials are the servants of the public; and the official must try not to foster the illusion that it is the other way round.

SIR ERNEST GOWERS (1880–1966)
Plain Words, 1948

He who serves the public hath but a scurvy master.

H.G. BOHN (1796–1884)
Handbook of Proverbs

High office is like a pyramid; only two kinds of animals reach the summit – reptiles and eagles.

D'ALEMBERT (1717–83)

Mr Hardlines ... was, perhaps, something of a Civil Service Pharisee ... if he could promote a movement beyond the walls of the Weights and Measures; if he could make Pharisees of those benighted publicans in the Strand; if he could introduce conic sections into the Custom House, and political economy into the Post Office; if by any effort of his, the Foreign Office clerks could be forced to attend punctually at ten; and that wretched saunterer, whom five days a week he saw laughing in the Council Office – if he could be made to mend his pace, what a wide field for his ambition would Mr Hardlines then have found! ... What if the Civil Service ... through his instrumentality, should become the nucleus of the best intellectual diligence in the country, instead of being a byword for sloth and ignorance!

ANTHONY TROLLOPE (1815–82)
The Three Clerks, 1857

Your public servants serve you right; indeed often they serve you better than your apathy or indifference deserve.

ADLAI EWING STEVENSON (1900–65)
1952

Show me the man who keeps his house in hand,
He's fit for public authority.
SOPHOCLES (496–406 BC)

I doubt whether any other country has so fully developed a committee system as Britain. Because no decision can be taken until every departmental interest has had its say, this system has a natural tendency to produce a soggy compromise.

DENIS HEALEY
The Time of my Life

The type of civil servant who has a difficulty for every solution.

A.E.W. THOMAS

The essential causes of Rome's decline lay in her people, her morals, her class struggle, her failing trade, her bureaucratic despotism, her stifling taxes, her consuming wars.

WILL DURANT
Caesar and Christ

Civil servants want to be loved. But one cannot love bureaucratic power. Only submit to it, fear it or hate it. Civil servants are the 'they' in our society.

DOUGLAS HOUGHTON
British politician

The State, in choosing men to serve it, takes no notice of their opinions. If they be willing faithfully to serve it, that satisfies.

OLIVER CROMWELL (1599–1658)
1644

Bureaucracy is based on a willingness either to pass the buck or to spend it.

MRS HENRY J. SERWAT

An official never flogs a bearer of gifts.

CHINESE PROVERB

The public official must pick his way nicely, must learn to placate though not to yield too much, to have the art of honeyed words but not to seem neutral, and above all to keep constantly audible, visible, likable, even kissable.

LEARNED HAND
speech in Washington, 1932

An official man is always an official man, and he has a wild belief in the value of reports.

SIR ARTHUR HELPS

Civil servants talk about politics as a yachts-
man might talk of the wind – a wild, irrational
force, always liable to upset the navigators'
calculations, yet having to be calculated for by
systems of tacking, reefing or battening down.

ANTHONY SAMPSON
The New Anatomy of Britain

The work of governing Lanchap has been
carried on quietly and with moderate efficiency
by the British Advisers – mostly colourless,
uxorious men with a taste for fishing or
collecting matchboxes or writing competent
monographs on the more accessible Malay
village customs.

ANTHONY BURGESS (1917–   )
Time For A Tiger, 1956

I had sitting with me a Committee representing all the departments concerned with the problem under consideration – all the best experts in the Government service – and very good experts they are.

    LORD BEVERIDGE
    1943

If the government is not right, then the sovereign's position is threatened, and when the sovereign's position is threatened, the powerful officials become arrogant and the minor officials begin to steal.

    CONFUCIUS (551–479 BC)

We must beware of trying to build a society in which nobody counts for anything except a politician or an official, a society where enterprise gains no reward and thrift no privileges.

    WINSTON CHURCHILL (1874–1965)
    1943

Roughly speaking, the official mind, then as now, was concerned to minimize any elements of unusualness, to deny as far as possible the fact of change and to preserve at all costs the appearance of legality. It is, in short, precedent-ridden, and already in the fourteenth century, if not earlier, the response of the civil servant to all difficulties was an order to search the rolls.

V.H. GALBRAITH
Studies in the Public Records

I get very fond of my civil servants (or at any rate some of them). The outside world has no idea how human they are.

BARBARA CASTLE
The Castle Diaries, 1974–76

You might as well have asked a jockey to become a totalizator clerk as expect Leamas to abandon operational life for the tendentious theorizing and clandestine self-interest of Whitehall.

JOHN LE CARRE (1931–   )
The Spy Who Came in from The Cold, 1963

The best upon the planet.

SENATOR MORTON (of Indiana)
on the American Civil Service

[US] Government service was speculative, and because of the opportunities it afforded attracted clever, sometimes brilliant men. Now it offers, in the main, the advantages of steady, light employment at a moderate remuneration and attracts the steadygoing and unimaginative.

C.R. FISH
The Civil Service and the Patronage

The Salary of the Doorkeeper of the Excise Office had been, by a scandalous job, raised to five hundred a year. It ought to have been reduced to fifty.

THOMAS BABINGTON MACAULEY (1800–59)
History of England, 1849–55

During the first half of the nineteenth century, the public services were filled with the nominees of peers and commoners who had votes in Parliament or weight in the constituencies. Since the privileged families were specially anxious to provide maintenance at the public expense for those of their members who were least likely to make their own way in life, the reputation of Whitehall for laziness and incompetence was proverbial. Heavy swells with long whiskers lounged in late and left early.

G.M. TREVELYAN (1876–1962)
British History in the Nineteenth Century and After

His abilities were precisely those which keep men long in power ... If he had been a man of original genius, and of a commanding mind, it would have been scarcely possible for him to keep his power, or even his head.

THOMAS BABINGTON MACAULEY (1800–59)
on Lord Burghley, Secretary of State to
Elizabeth I

... where everything is done through the bureaucracy, nothing to which the bureaucracy is really adverse can be done at all.

JOHN STUART MILL (1806–73)
On Liberty, 1859

We cannot meet it [the threat of dictatorship] if we turn this country into a wishy-washy imitation of totalitarianism, where every man's hand is out for pabulum and virile creativeness has given place to the patronizing favour of a swollen bureaucracy.

VANNEVAR BUSH
1949

The British bureaucrat has managed to transform inertia from a negative into a positive force. Bureaucracy is one huge 'sit tight' club.

SIR IAN HAMILTON
The Soul and Body of An Army

The working of great institutions is mainly the result of a vast mass of routine, petty malice, self interest, carelessness, and sheer mistake. Only a residual fraction is thought.

GEORGE SANTAYANA (1863–1952)
The Crime of Galileo

Now that the Cabinet's gone to its dinner,
The Secretary stays and gets thinner and thinner,
Racking his brains to record and report
What he thinks that they think they ought to have thought.

ANON

The State lies in all languages of good and evil.

FRIEDRICH NIETZSCHE (1844–1900)
Thus Spake Zarathustra, 1883–92

If public officers will infringe men's rights, they ought to pay greater damages than other men, to deter and hinder other officers from the like offenses.

LORD HOLT
1702

A situation in a public office is secure, but laborious and mechanical, and without the two great springs of life, Hope and Fear.

WILLIAM HAZLITT (1778–1830)
On the Conduct of Life

Bureaucracy, the rule of no one, has become the modern form of despotism.

MARY McCARTHY (1912–)
in the *New Yorker*, 1958

The British Civil Service is a beautifully designed and effective braking mechanism.

SHIRLEY WILLIAMS
1980

The executive of the modern State is but a committee for managing the common affairs of the whole bourgeoisie.

KARL MARX (1818–83) AND FRIEDRICH ENGELS (1820–95)
The Communist Manifesto, 1848

Tyranny is always better organized than freedom.

CHARLES PIERRE AEGUY

You do not need brains to be Minister of Transport because the Civil Servants have them.

ERNEST MARPLES
British politician

States are great engines moving slowly.

FRANCIS BACON (1561–1626)

Who works in the public square will have many advisers.

SPANISH PROVERB

The worth of a State, in the long run, is the worth of the individuals composing it.

> JOHN STUART MILL (1806–73)
> *On Liberty*, 1859

He was no fit counsellor to make your affairs better but yet he was fit to have kept them from getting worse.

> FRANCIS BACON (1561–1626)
> to James I on Robert Cecil, Lord Salisbury

It isn't accurate to say government 'is composed of' good people; government *is* simply people. They may be good people, but they are very bad wizards. Mortals have no magic.

> ROGER L. MACBRIDE
> *A New Dawn For America*

The worst thing that can be said about a civil servant is that he is emotional.

> RICHARD ADAMS
> in the *Radio Times*

One man's red tape is another man's system.

> DWIGHT WALDO
> *Elements of Public Administration*

The art of government is the organization of idolatry. The bureaucracy consists of functionaries; the aristocracy, of idols; the democracy, of idolaters. The populace cannot understand the bureaucracy: it can only worship the national idols.

GEORGE BERNARD SHAW (1856–1950)
Maxims for Revolutionists

Bureaucracy is the antithesis of democracy.

JO GRIMOND
British politician

We can overcome gravity, but sometimes the paperwork is overwhelming.

WERNHER VON BRAUN

States are made up of a considerable number of the ignorant and foolish, a small proportion of genuine knaves, and a sprinkling of capable and honest men, by whose efforts the former are kept in a reasonable state of guidance and the latter of repression.

T.H. HUXLEY (1825–95)
Administrative Nihilism

Every actual State is corrupt. Good men must not obey the laws too well. What satire on government can equal the severity of censure conveyed in the word *politic*, which now for ages has signified cunning, intimating that the State is a trick?

RALPH WALDO EMERSON (1803–82)
Politics

By non-usage all privileges are lost, say the clerks.

FRANCOIS RABELAIS (*c*. 1494– *c*. 1553)
Pantagruel, 1532 or 1533

Secrecy is the first essential in affairs of the State.

CARDINAL DE RICHELIEU (1585–1642)

Empires fall, ministries pass away, but bureaux remain.

DUC D'AUDIFFERT-PASQUIER

Whatever was required to be done, the Circumlocution Office was beforehand with all the public departments in the art of perceiving how not to do it.

CHARLES DICKENS (1812–70)
Little Dorrit, 1855–7

What is official
Is incontestable. It undercuts
The problematical world and sells us life
At a discount.

CHRISTOPER FRY (1907–   )
The Lady's Not For Burning, 1949

[Admission to the Civil Service was] eagerly sought, but it is only for the unambitious and the indolent or incapable that it is chiefly desired.

> NORTHCOTE/TREVELYAN
> report into the Civil Service, 1853

To administer is to govern: to govern is to reign. That is the essence of the problem.

> HONORÉ GABRIEL MIRABEAU (1749–1791)
> 1790

He who performs his duty in a station of great power must needs incur the utter enmity of many, and the high displeasure of more.

> ATTERBURY

The longer the title, the less important the job.

> GEORGE McGOVERN
> 1960

In a bureaucratic system, useless work drives out useful work.

> MILTON FRIEDMAN

To become a Chinese official it is necessary to be morally sound, honest, upright and enlightened. If persons possessing these qualities are not available, a selection is made from among others.

CHINESE OFFICIAL HANDBOOK

Serve and thou shalt be served. If you love and serve men, you cannot, by any hiding or stratagem, escape the remuneration.

RALPH WALDO EMERSON (1803–82)
Sovereignty of Ethics

It is certain that the services given to nations are held of far less account than those rendered to individuals.

FRANCESCO GUICCIARDINI (1483–1540)
Piu Consigli et Auvertimenti

The experience of anyone who has worked in Whitehall is that there is an early stage in any project when things are fluid; when, if you are in touch with those concerned and can get hold of the facts, it is fairly easy to influence decisions. But after the scheme has been worked on for weeks and months, and has hardened into a particular shape and come up for final decision, then it is very difficult to do anything except approve it or throw it overboard.

SIR EDWARD BRIDGES
'Whitehall and Beyond', *The Listener*, 1964

Of all the damnable waste of human life that ever was invented, clerking is the very worst.

GEORGE BERNARD SHAW (1856–1950)

Misalliance, 1910

What is a committee? A group of the unwilling, picked from the unfit, to do the unnecessary.

RICHARD HARKNESS

New York Herald Tribune, 1960

The function of the civil authority in the state is to protect and to foster, but by no means to absorb, the family and the individual, or to substitute itself for them.

POPE PIUS XI

Divini illius magistri

The foul, corruption-gender'd swarm of state.

ROBERT SOUTHEY (1774–1843)

Joan of Arc, 1796

Tariff: a scale of taxes on imports, designed to protect the domestic producer against the greed of his consumer.

AMBROSE BIERCE
The Devil's Dictionary

The government that is big enough to give you all you want is big enough to take it all away.

BARRY GOLDWATER,
1964

Frankly, I'd like to see the government get out of war altogether and leave the whole field to private industry.

JOSEPH HELLER
Catch-22

The greater part of what passes for diplomatic history is little more than the record of what one clerk said to another clerk.

GEORGE MALCOLM YOUNG
Victorian England: Portrait of an Age

It is unnecessary for a man to attend to public affairs without any interruption: such concentration is, indeed, more liable to render him useless than any other behaviour.

CARDINAL DE RICHELIEU
Chief Minister to Louis XIII, 1585–1642

*The
End*